Thomas Henseler and Susanne Buddenberg
Tunnel 57

PUBLICATION OF THE BERLIN WALL FOUNDATION

The comic "Tunnel 57" was made with the financial support of the Federal Foundation for the Reappraisel of the SED Dictatorship for a 2012 exhibition in the Bernauer Strasse metro station at the former border between West and East Berlin.

The German National Library catalogues this publication in the German National Bibliography; detailed bibliographical information available online at: www.dnb.de

First edition, April 2013
© Christoph Links Verlag GmbH
Schönhauser Allee 36, 10435 Berlin, Tel. +49 30 44 02 32-0
www.christoph-links-verlag.de; mail@christoph-links-verlag.de
Cover design: Michael Uszinski, with an illustration
from the comic "Tunnel 57"
Printed and bound: Bosch Druck, Landshut

ISBN 978-3-86153-729-8

Thomas Henseler and Susanne Buddenberg

Tunnel 57

A True Escape-Story

Translated by Rick Minnich

Ch. Links Verlag, Berlin

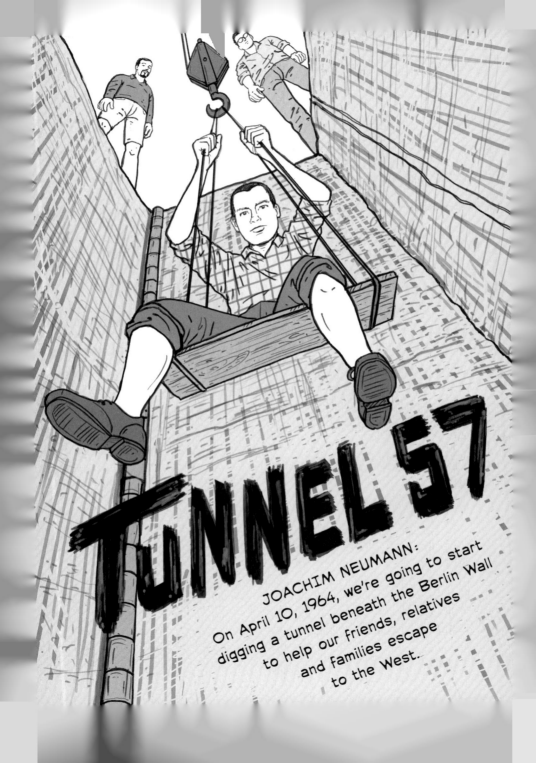

TUNNEL 57

JOACHIM NEUMANN:
On April 10, 1964, we're going to start digging a tunnel beneath the Berlin Wall to help our friends, relatives and families escape to the West.

WOLFGANG FUCHS, 25

is an acting student in West Berlin. Since 1962, he has organized the excavation of four escape tunnels. He is the leader of the group, and wants to bring more of his friends and relatives to the West.

HUBERT HOHLBEIN, 22

fled from Potsdam to West Berlin in 1963 by scuba diving across the Jungfernsee. He wants to bring his mother and other relatives to West Berlin through the tunnel.

JOACHIM NEUMANN, 25

I'm studying civil engineering. In 1961 I escaped to West Berlin. Since then, I've been waiting for an opportunity to bring my girlfriend Christa across. She's still being held in a Stasi prison for attempting to escape.

REINHARD FURRER, 24

is studying physics at the Free University in West Berlin. He wants to help a couple he knows in East Berlin escape to the West.

CHRISTIAN ZOBEL, 23

is studying medicine at the Free University in West Berlin. In 1956, his father was imprisoned in the East for suspected sabotage. After his family fled to the West, his father died as a consequence of prison conditions.

Another 20-25 people are involved in building the tunnel, and many more as messengers in charge of informing the refugees.

The tunnel begins in a shut-down bakery at Bernauer Strasse 97 (West). Wolfgang Fuchs used this spot once in January 1964 to build a tunnel which ended at a coal yard at Strelitzer Strasse 54 (East). Three women managed to escape at that time. The Stasi then discovered the tunnel and rendered it unusable. That's why a new tunnel is to be built.

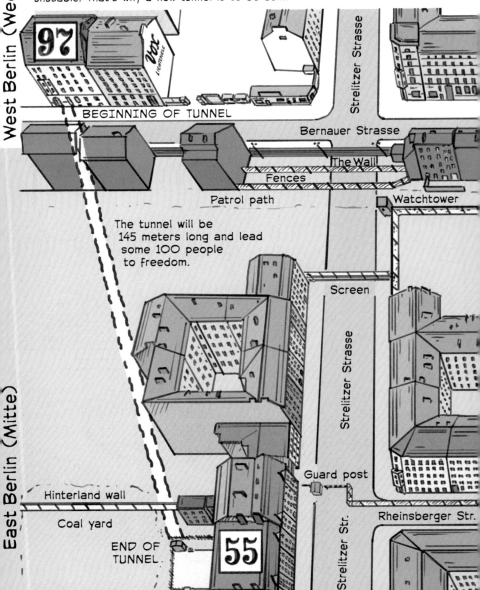

West Berlin (Wedding)

97

Vot LICHTSPIELE

BEGINNING OF TUNNEL

Strelitzer Strasse

Bernauer Strasse

The Wall

Fences

Patrol path

Watchtower

The tunnel will be 145 meters long and lead some 100 people to freedom.

Screen

Strelitzer Strasse

East Berlin (Mitte)

Guard post

Hinterland wall

Rheinsberger Str.

Coal yard

Strelitzer Str.

END OF TUNNEL

55

The work
is toilsome and
grueling.

↓

**12 m
deep**

During one 12-hour shift,
4–5 men can dig approximately
1–2 meters.

The rock and dirt are loaded onto a
rubber-wheeled wagon, which is pulled to
the tunnel shaft by a cable winch.

The wagon
is emptied in
the bakery
above.

RROOM RRRRRR

We dare to use an electric hammer only during the day, when cars and buses thunder over us. The risk is too great that border guards might hear the noise.

One shift lasts 14 days. Digging an 80 x 80 cm tunnel means surviving on thin air and virtually no daylight.

I use a theodolite to measure the direction and distance we need to go. This is not very accurate, and we have to correct our course several times.

Early October is the break-through.

After 6 months of tunneling, we finally reach the other side.

But where exactly?

We don't come out in the cellar of Strelitzer Strasse 55 as planned...

... but a few meters earlier...

...in a disused outhouse in the courtyard. We plan to open the tunnel the next evening.

The teddy bear was a present from Christa.

She'll recognize it immediately.

I give the bear to one of my roommates, Hartwig, and ask him to find a messenger for me. I've got to go open the tunnel.

The other messengers are already on their way to inform the escapees.

A few things all the escapees absolutely must bear in mind:

RASCHEL

RASCHEL
RASCHEL

No rustling clothes.

Walk on the right side of Strelitzer Strasse.

Our look-outs in West Berlin are keeping an eye on the area. If there's danger ahead, they'll flash the lights. This means: slowly return or turn into Rheinsberger Strasse.

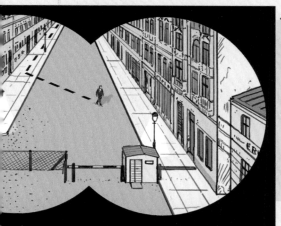

Cross from the right side of the street to the left so our look-outs can count the number of refugees.

Go to house number 55.

It is the next to last house before the barrier.

At the courtyard door whisper the password.

Tokyo...*

Take off your shoes.

I've got to take care of a few things here first. I'll come as soon as I can.

Step back.

Raise your hands and let your-self fall.

28 people – 6 men, 20 women, including Hubert Hohlbein's mother, and 2 children – escape on this day, October 3, 1964. The operations are to continue tomorrow.

Christa and I get married shortly thereafter.

END OF THE 1st ESCAPE DAY

DAY 2:

REINHARD FURRER: Listens to the refugees' password at the courtyard door, and points to the outhouse.

CHRISTIAN ZOBEL: Observes the approaching refugees through a crack in the door.

We all take up our usual positions:

HUBERT HOHLBEIN: Takes the refugees from me and lets them enter the tunnel.

JOACHIM NEUMANN: I take over the refugees in front of the outhouse.

The West Berlin police supply us with gas masks to protect ourselves against possible Stasi gas grenades.

We're all carrying guns. They are to be used only in an absolute emergency.

The lookouts with the aliases PEA and BEAN are stationed at Strelitzer Strasse 46 and Bernauer Strasse 93. Their task is to monitor the eastern side of Strelitzer Strasse. They have walkie-talkie contact with SAUCEPAN at the bakery.

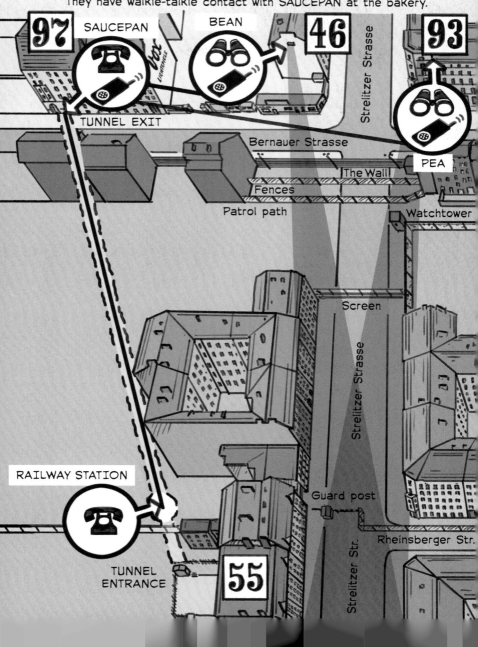

8 P.M.

Another 29 refugees are scheduled to flee through the tunnel tonight.

10:45 P.M.

The Ministry of State Security is tipped off
that a tunnel escape is in full swing.

STIEL   NAGEL

Based on the informant's statement,
Captain Stiel and Major Nagel reckon
that the tunnel must be near
Schönhauser Allee

They recall a foiled tunnel
escape at a coal yard
at Strelitzer
Strasse 54

Because the door to number 54 is locked, they try to reach the coal yard through the adjoining building, number 55.

They rattle at the large court-yard door. Locked.

QUICK! TURN OFF THE LIGHTS!

THIS WAY! TAKE OFF YOUR SHOES!

We can't go yet. We've got to fetch a friend!

He just got out of prison and is afraid to come here alone!

One of you can leave. The other stays here.

No can do! We'll be right back!

Strange guys!

I don't like this at all!

We wait for information from "Saucepan".

How long should the tunnel stay open?

Up to now, we've helped 57 refugees escape to the West through the tunnel.

12:30 A.M. A sound in the hallway.

Several people come through the door.

Reinhard Furrer goes to meet the presumed refugees...

A machine gun?!

"DANGER! DANGER!"

Our lookout's telephone warning cry no longer reaches us.

COME WITH US!

COCK YOUR GUNS!

Panic-stricken, Hohlbein, Furrer and I get wedged in the narrow tunnel.

We crawl back through the tunnel in mortal fear.

LIFT US UP!

LIFT US UP!

Fearing Stasi gas grenades, we fill up the tunnel in panic.

Then Christian Zobel leaps down onto us and loosens our knot.

Christian is really troubled that he, a medical student, fired at someone in self-defense.

How do you know you hit somebody?

I heard a loud groan.

He would never recover.

For the next few days, the tunnel escape is all over the newspapers:

WESTERN PRESS

 Escape Helper Shot in Self-Defense

DIE WELT

Protest against Shooting of Sergeant Schultz

Telegraf

57 People are Happy
200 m Tunnel underneath Bernauer Strasse

Bild Hail of Bullets at Escape Tunnel – VOPO* Killed

57 Made it Through!

*VOPO = Volkspolizist (East German policeman)

BERLINER MORGENPOST

Four Tunnel Diggers Surrender to Public Prosecutor
VOPO Egon Schultz Shot in Self-Defense

EASTERN PRESS

NEUES DEUTSCHLAND
ORGAN DES ZENTRALKOMITEES DER SOZIALISTISCHEN EINHEITSPARTEI DEUTSCHLANDS

Sergeant Egon Schultz Murdered by West Berlin Agent

Berliner Zeitung

Villainous Murder of Border Guard

Junge Welt

Outrage at Cowardly Assassination

NEUES DEUTSCHLAND
ORGAN DES ZENTRALKOMITEES DER SOZIALISTISCHEN EINHEITSPARTEI DEUTSCHLANDS

GDR Attorney General Demands Extradition of Murderers

BZ am Abend **Provocation Consciously Staged**

At Last, Preliminary Proceedings Against the Murderer of Sergeant Schultz

Egon Schultz, 21, is given a state funeral.

More than 100 schools, orphanages, holiday hotels and other establishments in the East are named after him.

East Germany demands the extradition of the "murderers."

The West Berlin prosecuting authorities request the forensics report.

The highly-esteemed Prof. Dr. med. Otto Prokop, head of forensic medicine at the Charité Hospital in East Berlin, was instructed to perform the autopsy.

The East German state security service conducts a forensic examination at the scene of the crime. They discover the following:

Reinhard Furrer ran to the tunnel entrance.

Captain Stiel and Sergeant Egon Schultz entered the courtyard.

Christian Zobel was standing at the gateway...

...and fired several shots.

Prof. Prokop comes to the conclusion that it wasn't the escape helper's shot that killed Egon Schultz but rather the salvo from the border guard''s Kaláshnikov.

MINISTERIUM FÜR STAATS...

Top secret!
Return after use!

The Ministry of State Security keeps the true cause of death under wraps for decades.

Only after the fall of the Berlin Wall in 1989 does the truth come out.

Memorial plaque for Egon Schultz during the GDR regime:

ON OCTOBER 5, 1964 IN THE HALLWAY OF THIS HOUSE

SERGEANT

EGON SCHULTZ

BORN ON JANUARY 4, 1943

WAS ASSASSINATED BY WEST BERLIN AGENTS WHILE FULFILLING HIS DUTIES TO PROTECT THE NATIONAL BORDER OF THE GERMAN DEMOCRATIC REPUBLIC.

Plaque in Strelitzer Strasse 55 today:

In the courtyard of this building ended a 145 m long tunnel dug from West Berlin through which 57 men, women and children escaped to the West during the nights of October 3–4, 1964. After the escape was betrayed to the Ministry of State Security of the GDR, border guards and escape helpers exchanged fire.

Egon Schultz
Sergeant in the border troops of the National People's Army
* January 4, 1943 in Gross–Jestin (Kr. Kolberg)

lost his life on October 5th. In the GDR, Egon Schultz was idealized as a hero; the escape helpers were considered agents and murderers. Only after the fall of the Berlin Wall was it made public that the deadly shots were fired by one of Schultz's own comrades. GDR authorities were aware of this fact all along.

THE END

The comic "Tunnel 57" is based on a true story.

Wolfgang Fuchs
was one of the best known and most successful escape helpers.

Hubert Hohlbein
completed his studies and worked as an electrical engineer.

Reinhard Furrer
became a physics professor and one of the first Germans in space. In October 1985, he traveled with seven other astronauts aboard the Space Shuttle Challenger, and conducted various physics experiments on board. In 1995, he suffered fatal injuries in an air show at the Johannisthal Air Field in Berlin.

Christian Zobel
became a doctor. The thought that he killed the border sergeant Egon Schultz haunted him throughout his life. He died in the early 1990s, unaware that he was not a murderer.

Joachim Neumann
participated in the construction of six different tunnels before helping his girl-friend escape to the West through "Tunnel 57". After completing his studies in civil engineering, he worked on large tunnel projects in numerous countries.

Scenario, drawings and gray tones:
Thomas Henseler and Susanne Buddenberg
Zoom und Tinte Buddenberg und Henseler GbR
All rights reserved
Financial support provided by The Federal Foundation for the Reappraisel of the SED Dictatorship

Historical consultant:
Dr. Maria Nooke – Berlin Wall Memorial

Many thanks to our eyewitnesses:
Joachim Neumann, Hubert Hohlbein, Dr. Peter Schulenburg, Klaus-M. von Keussler

Literature referenced:
Klaus-M. von Keussler / Peter Schulenburg:
Fluchthelfer – Die Gruppe um Wolfgang Fuchs. Berlin Story Verlag, Berlin 2011

Typesetting and graphic design:
Andreas Rupprecht

English translation:
Rick Minnich

Thomas Henseler and Susanne Buddenberg studied design at the Fachhochschule Aachen and film at the Hochschule für Film und Fernsehen "Konrad Wolf" in Potsdam-Babelsberg. Upon completing their studies, they founded the company "Zoom und Tinte Buddenberg und Henseler GbR", which specializes in film and illustration. Zoom und Tinte work in the fields of comics, illustration and storyboarding. Thomas Henseler and Susanne Buddenberg also teach design, film and game design. They have previously published two other historical comics about East German history: "Grenzfall" (2011) and "BERLIN – A City Divided" (2012).

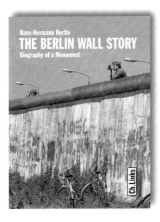

Hans-Hermann Hertle
The Berlin Wall Story
Biography of a Monument

248 pages · 169 illustrations · softcover · pocket-size
ISBN 978-3-86153-650-5
4,90 € (D)

Where did the Berlin Wall actually stand? Why was it built? How did people keep managing to escape across it – and how many died in the attempt? Why did it come down in the end? Numerous previously unknown photographs document the construction of this barrier system of barbed wire, alarm fences and concrete. Spectacular escape stories and shocking deaths are chronicled here in words and images, as are the dramatic events surrounding the construction and the fall of the Wall. A stunning survey of the Berlin Wall – the central symbol of the Cold War.

Hans-Hermann Hertle · Maria Nooke (Hg.)
The Victims at the Berlin Wall 1961 – 1989
A Biographical Handbook

512 pages · 117 illustrations · hardcover
ISBN 978-3-86153-632-1
24,90 € (D)

Although many deaths at the Berlin Wall have been publicized over the years in the media, the number, identity and fate of the victims still remain largely unknown. This handbook changes this by answering the following questions: How many people actually died at the Berlin Wall between 1961 and 1989? Who were these people? How did they die? How were their relatives and their friends treated after their deaths? What public and political reactions were triggered in the East and the West by these fatalities? What were the consequences for the border guards who pulled the trigger and the military and political leaders who gave them their orders after the East German border regime collapsed and the Wall fell? How have the victims been commemorated since their deaths?
By documenting the lives and circumstances under which these men and women died at the Wall, these deaths are placed in a contemporary historical context. The authors, in addition to systematically researching the relevant archives and examining all the legal proceedings and Stasi documents, also conducted interviews with family members and contemporary witnesses.

Ch. Links Verlag · Schönhauser Allee 36 · 10435 Berlin · www.christoph-links-verlag.de

Ch.Links